CURTAIN INSPIRATION

A source book of pictures and ideas

CURTAIN INSPIRATION

A source book of pictures and ideas

Catherine Merrick & Rebecca Day

Photographs by Michael Beard
Edited by Caroline Brandenburger

CURTAIN INSPIRATION

For Geoffrey and Nicholas

ISBN 0 9535267-3-9

Reproduction by Radstock Reprographics
Printed and bound in Great Britain by Butler & Tanner Ltd
Frome and London

Photographer: Michael Beard
Editor: Caroline Brandenburger
Jacket design: Richard Hannaford

Merrick & Day
Redbourne Hall, Redbourne, Gainsborough, Lincolnshire, DN21 4JG England
Telephone:+44(0)1652 648814 Facsimile:+44(0)1652 648104
Email: sales@merrick-day.com Website: www.merrick-day.com

Acknowledgments

Our sincerest thanks go to Betty, Glynnis, Lynn and Pauline, also Brenda, who have made up the vast majority of the curtains pictured in this book, a great achievement; also Anne and Catherine for all their work too. Thanks as well to those curtain and blind makers, unknown to us, whose curtains and blinds we came across in the course of photography and could not resist including.

None of this would have been possible without our clients and interior designers, particularly Sue Dyson and Carolyn Holmes. Again, thank you. Everyone was so kind and hospitable when we visited their homes to take photographs.

Many thanks as well to Mike Beard for his outstanding photographs; for his skill, energy, constant good nature and being a real pleasure to work with. And his wife Jessica who assisted on several shoots. Huge thanks to Caroline Brandenburger, the editor, for her enthusiasm, flair, perserverance, salad lunches and always being able to come up with the appropriate word. Thanks to her husband Charles for his forbearance. Thank you to Richard and Diane Hannaford for all their helpful comments and for Richard's elegant cover design.

Thanks to colleagues, friends and family who have taken the time to comment on drafts of this book throughout its various stages. Finally, we would like to thank our husbands Geoffrey and Nicholas, our children Amy, Minnie, Rebecca, Augustus, William and Katie, and also Mother and Father for their constant support.

Thanks to the following for kindly allowing photography:

Mr and Mrs R Abbott
Albany House Antiques, Horncastle
Mr and Mrs P Arden
Ash Interiors
Mr and Mrs J Bacon
Mr and Mrs E Bedford
Mr and Mrs J Cooper
Mr and The Hon Mrs S Blackett
Mr and Mrs R Borrill
Mr and Mrs D Chambers
Mr and Mrs JO Day
Mrs C Doughty
Sue Dyson Interiors
Mr & Mrs R Elwes
Mr and Mrs S Foster
Mr and Mrs D Goose

Mr and Mrs M Hencher
Mr and Mrs W Herring
Carolyn Holmes Interiors
Mr and Mrs T Jones
Mr and Mrs C Kenyon
Mr and Mrs G Maitland-Smith
Mr and Mrs N Marshall
Mr and Mrs S Merrick
Mr and Mrs W Rigley
Mr and Mrs B Rowles
Mr and Mrs W Sleeman
Mr and Mrs R Stables
Mr and Mrs ATG Turnbull
Mrs and Mrs J Vernam
Mr and Mrs D Whyles
Mr and Mrs A Woodhouse

Picture credits:
Sue Dyson and June Ash of Ash Interiors, Jersey
p.35 Top left, p.117,Below, p.181 Right.

Sue Dyson of Sue Dyson Interiors, London
Front cover photograph, pp.26-27, p.36,
p.57 Right, pp.62-69, pp.98-99, p.117, p.136,
pp.178-179, p.180 Left.

Carolyn Holmes of Carolyn Holmes Interiors
pp.12-13, pp.22-25, pp.28-29, p.37, p.41,
p.51 Right, p.59 Below, p.60 Right, pp.74-75,
pp.76-77 Centre, pp.78-79, p.91, pp.96-97,
pp.100-101, p.106 Right, pp.107-110, p.116,
p.117 Top, p.125-126, p.128, p.137, p.139 Top,
p.144 Left, pp.164-165, pp.176-177.

Introduction

This book is here to inspire you.

There are hundreds of photographs of all sorts of room settings, window shapes and treatments, all intended to give you inspiration and ideas for your home or project. You may reproduce exactly what you see in the picture, curtains, swags and tails complete. Or you may draw only on the simplest element, just a way of trimming, or holding back a curtain.

After all, dressing windows is crucial for the success of a room. Not only for its aesthetic appeal, but for comfort and practicality. There is always more than one way of dressing a window. Use this book as a starting point to understand the options and to find the ideal solution.

As with all our books, *Curtain Inspiration* has arisen directly from our own experience as curtain makers. We started making curtains more than a decade ago, and realised what a variety and range of window treatments we have created over the years for different clients. *Curtain Inspiration* shows a good deal of that range and variety.

The book is divided into four clear sections. ROOM SETTINGS shows different ways of treating the windows in all the main rooms of the home. WINDOW TYPES illustrates a variety of ways of approaching a wide range of window shapes. CURTAIN STYLES demonstrates the range of window treatments from simple curtains and sheers to elaborate swags and tails. BLINDS & SHUTTERS shows how you can stylishly dress a window with something other than a curtain and also completes the book.

Curtains are infinite in their possibilities, but whether you live in the town or the country, in a flat or a house, embrace the traditional or the modernist, there will be something for you in *Curtain Inspiration*.

Catherine and Rebecca, Redbourne, September 2001

NOTE: For guidance on how to make many of the window treatments featured in this book, help is at hand in another of our publications, *The Encyclopaedia of Curtains*.

Contents

ROOM SETTINGS

HALLS, STAIRS & LANDINGS

YOUR HALL creates the first impression of your home for visitors. Here is an opportunity for drama and a flourish, especially as some hall and landing windows are very tall. Then there are practical considerations, such as a door curtain for heat conservation, or maximising light in a dark hall. Often challenging, the hall, stairs and landing windows may be an assortment of shapes and sizes. Continuity can be achieved by using the same fabric and trimmings, while the style of curtain can be varied to suit the window.

LEFT An imposing window in a grand entrance hall; it demands an imposing treatment. The fabric chosen is a bold tapestry style. A deep arch-shaped valance with long French pleats hangs from a substantial reeded wooden pole. This dramatic valance is trimmed with chenille tassel fringe, the leading edges and overlong hems are finished with hand-sewn chenille rope.

ABOVE A close-up of the elegant carved and gilded finial and decorative pole bracket.

LEFT The curtain is held back by a sumptuous chenille rope tie-back which coordinates with the fringe on the valance and the rope on the leading edges and hems.

LEFT A single, paisley fabric, tab-headed curtain hangs from a pole, fitted in the recess, and is held by a tassel tieback.

ABOVE A detail of the tab heading.

RIGHT A Roman blind hangs at the porch window, the blind is made up in corduroy fabric and bound, on three sides, in the same paisley fabric as the door curtain for continuity.

BELOW Detail of corduroy blind with its paisley edge.

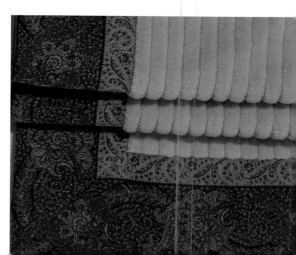

FAR RIGHT An impressive double-height hall window and a half-landing window, both with gathered-headed curtains hanging from substantial wooden poles. The poles have ball-end finials to echo the ball ends on the newel posts, and are stained to match the panelling. Wool fabric and wide staircase permits soft pooling on the floor. Chenille mix bobble fringe adds a lively touch on the leading edges.

RIGHT A head-on view of the double-height hall window. The window seat and cushions give the window and hall a comfortable look.

FAR RIGHT INSET The same hall and stair windows pictured in the 1940's. Note the carefully thought-out detail, the equivalent height of braid trim on both the small and the large window links the two. In contrast to today's floor-length treatment, then the longer curtains were cut to the shortest point of contact with the stairs.

The higher the ceiling, the thicker the poles should be, in general terms. Here, the wooden poles are 7.5cm (3in) diameter, to relate to the 6.5m(21ft) ceiling height. Of course, the weight of the fabric in such long curtains requires extra-secure bracket fixings.

LEFT A stairwell window in a family home with full-length curtains which avoid the hazard of tripping. The curtains are combined with classic swags, tails and a centre trumpet; they are all trimmed with bullion fringe.

TOP Curtains by day; the left-hand curtain has been cut away at the hem to accommodate the shape of the step.

ABOVE Curtains by night; the cut-away hem flows elegantly when drawn at night.

Curtains on stairs often have the added problem of accommodating the change in levels of the steps. When this is the case, the options are: sill-length curtains; full-length curtains to the shortest point of contact with the stairs; over-long curtains as on the previous double page; or ingenious cut-away hems to accommodate the steps as shown in the pictures above.

ABOVE Arched, stair window with full-length curtains and gathered valance. The lower edge of the valance is shaped to follow the curve of the arched window and trimmed with bullion fringe. The top of the valance has a small contrast binding and rope trim sewn along the gather line.

RIGHT A view from the hall up the stairs showing the hemlines that have been cut to the shortest point of contact with the stairs.

DRAWING ROOMS & SITTING ROOMS

HERE, IT is all a question of atmosphere. A drawing room will want to be comfortable, peaceful, and suitable for entertaining guests, while a sitting room is for relaxing with the family, enjoying television and more informal entertaining. In either case, maximum light is important for a sunny, lively atmosphere by day. Choose from the full range of window treatments, from immaculately cut and fringed swags and tails to simple blinds.

LEFT Beautiful, formal drawing-room, with sumptuous striped silk taffeta curtains and a hand-smocked valance. The curtains and valance hang from an elegant curved, shaped pelmet board.

ABOVE A brass ombra used here on the outside of the curtain as a fabulous tie-back hook.

LEFT Close-up of one of the specially-made, double-tassel tie-backs, which matches the bullion fringe used on the smock-headed valance.

ABOVE A matching pair of drawing-room windows sumptuously dressed in lavish ball-gown style. The valances and curtains are treble fullness and overlong for a dramatically opulent effect. The curtains are finished with a silk fan edging on the leading edges.

These over-long curtains add drama. The curtains are 30cm (12in) over-long for an opulent effect. However, extra length for curtains can be from as little as 2.5cm (1in) to 10cm (4in).

RIGHT A close-up of the hand-sewn smocked-headed valance, trimmed with silk bullion fringe, hanging from a shaped pelmet board. There are five rows of hand smocking, sewn with embroidery silks, which create a decorative honeycomb effect.

FAR LEFT A rich, warm drawing room where the window treatment effectively combines an unusual mix of textures and fabrics. The over-the-pole, formally cut swags and tails are made up in red-and-gold striped silk. The tails are lined in yellow silk, and all trimmed with gold chenille bullion fringe. The curtains are made up in a self-patterned chenille and held by chenille rope and tassel tie-backs.

LEFT A narrow French window in the same room. For ease of access there is a single curtain rather than a pair. The curtain is balanced by the long and short tail, and only one swag is draped over the short pole.

BELOW Close-up of finial.

When a pole is draped with swags, and the curtains need to be opened and closed, simply hang the curtains from a working track fitted behind and below the pole. To avoid the curtains disturbing the swags, project the pole forwards by fixing the pole brackets onto wooden blocks. The projected pole will create a gap at the sides, which can be concealed by extending the side of the tail.

ABOVE Bay window with working shutters and dress curtains hanging from poles. In the evenings, the shutters rather than the dress curtains are closed for privacy and warmth.

ABOVE LEFT Close-up of pole, finial and inverted box-pleated heading.

LEFT Close-up of natural jute double-tassel tie-back.

RIGHT Stylish London drawing-room in creams and neutrals, highlighted with black. Box-pleated cream curtains have wide, 5cm (2in), contrast leading edges and hems, and are held back by jute tassel tie-backs. Tie-backs also hang at the ends of the black poles, which are finished with ribbed and gilded ball end finials. The natural jute contrasts cleverly with the sophistication of the curtain fabric.

ABOVE Detail of valance with coronet, trumpet and knotted rope. The valance has a green contrast binding at the top and fringe on the lower edge.

The trumpet has been made separately, sewn onto the valance and the join covered by hand-sewn knotted rope.

RIGHT An elegant drawing room with pretty chintz curtains and valances at all three windows. The gathered valances with trumpets are set onto flat yokes at the top edges and have gently curved and fringed lower edges; they all hang from serpentine-shaped pelmet boards.

ABOVE A cream Roman blind with an attractive, woven patterned fabric border on three sides. The blind fits neatly in the window recess creating a back drop for the bronze busts by day and by night.

LEFT Close-up of the edge of the contrast-bound blind.

RIGHT A bright sitting room with a Roman blind hanging at the small window on the right-hand side and single curtains hanging from iron poles, which have been fitted above glazed doors, at either side of the fire place. The curtains are goblet headed and the leading edges are trimmed with the same fabric as the blind.

LEFT A cosy sitting-room with a bold colour scheme. The windows were challenging; the left-hand window had a lot of wall space above it, and a radiator below it, while the right-hand window had no wall space above at all. The solution was a Roman blind fitted on the wall space above the small window on the left, and a narrow pole with a deep puffed heading on the larger window. The Roman blind was related to the curtain by unusually applying a deep puffed heading at the top, which softened the tailored effect.

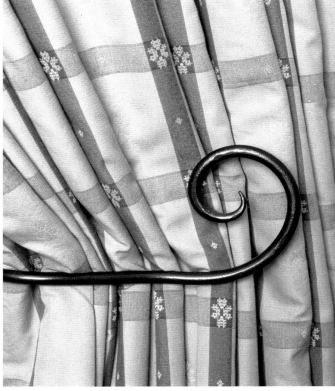

TOP A detail of the attractive curtain puffed heading.

ABOVE An iron hold-back which matches the curtain pole.

LEFT A closer view of the Roman blind finished with an attached puffed heading to match the curtain.

DINING ROOMS & KITCHENS

FOR ENTERTAINING, formal dining rooms need to strike a balance between drama and practical comfort. They are places of conversation and conviviality. Generous curtains and bold colour schemes can be used to create atmosphere, whether by day or by night. While dining kitchens, often the hub of the home, are more relaxed and by their very nature need to be more practical and light; simple, bright and cheerful are the keynotes.

LEFT An intimate formal dining room. The cream silk curtains have check contrast-bound leading edges and tops and are hanging from reeded, dark mahogany poles. The cream curtains are foil for the strong red walls and mahogany furniture.

ABOVE A close-up of one of the dark mahogany vase-shaped finials.

LEFT A close-up of the check silk taffeta contrast binding, and the hand-gathered curtain heading hanging from a reeded wooden pole.

ABOVE Classic dining room with classic swags and tails in a red-and-gold bold striped fabric. Four curtains have been used to dress this impressive Georgian bay window. Unusually, the stripes run across the swags rather than vertically as in the curtains. Cream roller blinds are hung behind the curtains to protect the silk curtains and furniture from the sunlight.

ABOVE RIGHT Dining room with traditional furniture and cheerful blue-check curtains that combine brightly with the sunny yellow walls. The goblet-headed curtains hang from elegant curved pelmet boards and are held open by high tassel tie-backs. Rope is knotted at the base of the goblets and rope and tassels are hung at the centre of the curtains.

RIGHT A bay window in this elegant dining room, deep arched valances are gathered onto flat yokes with rope clovers and tassels at either end.

FAR RIGHT Single window in the same dining room.

FAR RIGHT ABOVE A close-up of the tri-coloured bullion fringe on valances.

ABOVE A smart town dining room with simple cream curtains, Venetian blinds and upholstered striped flat pelmet. The pelmet conceals the blind when it is pulled up.

RIGHT A view through the modern wooden shutters which connect the kitchen to the dining room.

FAR RIGHT An untrimmed Roman blind made up in a large check fabric is fitted neatly into the window recess, and completes the inviting cafe effect.

LEFT Light and airy dining area. At the large sliding windows, French-pleated curtains hang from a slim chrome pole. Contemporary finials add a distinctive finish. At the small window with the radiator below it, a Roman blind.

ABOVE A close-up of the Roman blind that has been fitted up to the ceiling on the wall space above the window; no light is lost.

RIGHT Close-up of French pleats.

For ease of access, the pole extends well beyond the sliding windows. The curtains are French-pleated, as this heading stacks back more compactly than other curtain headings.

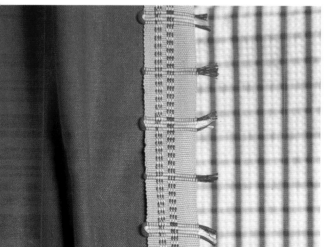

ABOVE Hanging from black iron poles, these deep red curtains contrast dramatically with the dark green walls in this country dining-kitchen. The window above the radiator has full-length dress curtains and a working Roman blind fitted in the window recess. Working curtains hang at the French windows.

LEFT Detail of braid on the curtain's leading edge with check blind behind.

A small pleated/cartridge heading with little fullness shows the large tulip patterned fabric to its best advantage.
The French window curtains hang just above the ground to keep them clean.

ABOVE A bay window with an iron pole following the bay's shape. The pole is supported by side brackets and a specially-made, heavy-duty centre bracket to take the weight of the interlined curtains.

RIGHT Close-up of finial and gathered heading with mock ties.

BEDROOMS & BATHROOMS

YOUR BEDROOM should be a tranquil place, private and away from everyday life. Curtain design and fabric should promote that peaceful atmosphere, and on a more practical note, must filter, even exclude light while providing warmth and privacy. Bedroom window treatments present an opportunity to indulge in a softer, prettier look if that is your style. Bathroom window treatments tend to be simpler.

LEFT A four-poster bed dressed with magnificent Italian-strung curtains at each corner. The curtains have a fringe on the leading edges, are lined in a contrasting fabric and held back to the bed posts at mattress level by tassel tie-backs. The bed posts are antique and mounted onto a large modern frame, as antique four-poster frames tend to be small by today's standards.

ABOVE Detail of chintz curtain fabric.

LEFT Close-up of the custom-made double-tassel tie-back that holds back the bed curtain. The skirts of the tie-back tassels are finished with small coloured tassels.

ABOVE A close-up view of the cream chintz pleated ceiling finished in the centre with a chou. The bed curtains and shallow valance are trimmed with a pretty tri-coloured fan-edging. Here, a wooden frame with cross-stretchers for support was made, then cream fabric was pleated onto it to create a ceiling for the bed. Small tracks were fitted around the frame for the valance and the side and back bed curtains to hang from.

RIGHT Traditional chintz-dressed four-poster bed. For a united look, the curtains, valances and bed valance are all made up in the same chintz. Black-out blinds hang behind the curtains.

All four-posters are different in their construction. Fittings and treatments need to be individually tailored to suit the frame. The important consideration is that fittings and curtain hooks should be concealed.

ABOVE Dramatic carved wooden four-poster bed dressed only with a back curtain, stretched ceiling and shallow valance, showing the damask and carving off to best advantage.

RIGHT Close-up of the top of the bed with its flat damask ceiling.

The absence of side curtains allows the light from the table lamps to be used for reading in bed. When there are side curtains, wall lamps on swing arms can be fitted inside the bed.

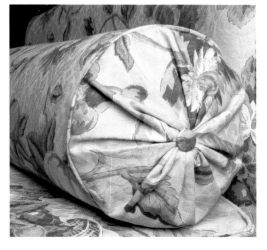

ABOVE The curtains are slotted on to poles. The curtains have a generous stand-up frill above the slot and are trimmed with fringe on the leading edges. Roller blinds fitted in the window recesses complete the effect.

LEFT A close-up of the bolster cushion.

When making slot-headed curtains that are pushed onto poles, the depth of the machined channel needs to be twice the diameter of the pole so it can be slotted through easily.

ABOVE A corner of a charming bedroom. Puff-headed, dress curtains are permanently held in position at the front of the dormer. A functional Roman blind in a contrasting fabric with an attached puffed heading is fitted in the window recess.

RIGHT A close-up of the inside ceiling of the Polonaise bed. The bed curtains are wholly supported by the shaped metal frame which is screwed firmly to the wooden bed frame.

FAR RIGHT A free-standing, Polonaise bed, which reaches right up to the ceiling, has been placed centrally in the same bedroom. The bed hangings are in the same chintz fabric as the curtains, and contrast-lined in plain fabric. At each corner the hangings are held by double-tassel tie-backs, and the top of the bed is finished with four small swags trimmed with fringe. The spectacular fringe is made from wooden balls, which are graduated in size, and covered in silk yarn.

FAR LEFT AND LEFT An antique brass corona suspended from a hook in the ceiling. It is dressed with muslin curtains trimmed with bobble fringe and held back by silk rope ties. The corona is decorated with old silk violets. The light-weight muslin back curtain is weighted at the hem with a metal rod to ensure it hangs straight.

BELOW An eighteenth-century embroidered curtain pelmet used, to good effect, as a modern hanging above this simple white bed.

RIGHT Green-and-cream, check puff-headed curtains hang from a fabric-covered lath at this small window.

BELOW RIGHT Detail of the bed cover.

FAR LEFT BELOW A sunny and warm bedroom. Creamy yellow silk curtains hang from shaped pelmet boards, with inner muslin curtains behind, which soften the leading edges. The hand-smocked headed valances have a contrast top and fringe along the lower edge. A pretty toile-de-jouy bed cover and day bed add to the delightful effect.

FAR LEFT ABOVE Details of one of the inner muslin curtains trimmed with linen fan edge; fringe with braid top; two rows of coloured hand smocking (the colours have been taken from the coloured braid on the cut fringe) and contrast binding on the top of valance.

LEFT The same window treatment has been repeated successfully in the comfortable adjoining dressing room.

ABOVE An Austrian blind on a small window in the bathroom next door, again using the same fabrics, fringe and smock heading.

These shaped pelmet boards were made extra deep to accommodate two working tracks, one for the main curtains and one for the inner muslin curtains.

ABOVE A Roman blind is a practical choice for this bathroom window.

LEFT A spacious bathroom adjoining the bedroom on the previous page.

To avoid splashing window treatments, make sure they are hung away from taps. Unless the bathroom is large, keep curtains or blinds simple with minimal fabric.

ABOVE A pretty feminine bathroom for relaxing in. A working roller blind is set behind a chintz London blind.

London blinds are a crisp variation on the Austrian blind theme. They are not gathered and full as Austrian blinds are. The fabric is flat except for the pleats where it is drawn up.

RIGHT A light calm bathroom in the country which is not overlooked. A simple antique lace panel covers half the window, allowing the bather to lie back and enjoy the rural outlook. The lace curtain has a channel heading slotted onto a net wire. The net wire is fitted simply to the window frame with hooks and screw eyes.

LEFT A stunning pair of eyelet-headed shower curtains attached to a chrome circular rail, flamboyantly placed in the centre of this shower room.

ABOVE AND TOP An eyelet-headed shower curtain hangs from a pole; cotton curtains hang from short tracks.

CHILDREN'S ROOMS

ROOMS FOR CHILDREN are an opportunity to let your imagination run free. A chance for bold use of colour and imagery to reflect your child's personality and stage of development. Simple curtains can be used to great effect and easily changed in the next make-over. Here, you can indulge in fantastic themes and have fun!

LEFT Vibrantly coloured sill-length curtains in this child's playroom. The tasselled curtain fabric and contrasting flat scalloped pelmet contribute to the playful effect.

ABOVE Gathered unlined velour curtains trimmed with red loops on the hem, hang from a white pole.

LEFT A Roman blind made from sari fabric for a fashionable teenage girl's bedroom. The edge of the blind has been finished with sari border.

LEFT At this dormer window double-sided curtains with very little fullness are slotted onto black iron dormer rods. The window architrave and sill have been painted to match the curtain fabric to great effect.

RIGHT An artful use of children's plaid fringed blankets to make cosy curtains for this playroom. These curtains are easy to construct, and are attached to the curtain rings with clips. The window architrave and sill are painted the same colour as the pole, shelf and skirting boards for a cohesive look.

ABOVE A Roman blind made from team-coloured stripe fabric for an aspiring young footballer. It is set in the recess of this dormer window.

Curtain fittings for children need to be securely fixed and easily opened and closed. Curtain cords can be dangerous and with small children, best avoided.

MODERN CLASSICS

THIS CONTEMPORARY look embraces simplicity, clear lines, neutral colours and natural materials and fabrics. Athough the style is modern, it has an enduring, timeless quality. The curtains and blinds act as a foil for the furniture and other furnishings. Plain or linear fabrics in cotton or linen made into unfussy window treatments work well with modern, clean-lined furniture.

LEFT Simple cream cotton curtains with a suede contrast-bound leading edge and a striking striped suede and cotton box-pleated valance which relates well to the strong lines of the furniture in this bedroom. A wooden Venetian blind adds visual warmth as well as privacy.

ABOVE A juxtaposition of textures. A detail of the wooden Venetian blind and the suede-trimmed cotton curtain.

LEFT A view of the bedroom curtains and blind from the corridor.

LEFT Plain cream French-headed curtains hang from a corded pole and are held back by ombras.

RIGHT In the connecting sitting room, for continuity, a pair of similar windows are treated in an identical manner to the dining room.

ABOVE A close-up of the finial and decorative bracket and also a detail of the barley-twist, dark mahogany pole highlighted with gold which is hung with French-headed curtains.

Corded poles are the solution when curtains hung from a pole are made in delicate fabric and should not be handled. A track can be inserted in a groove on the underside of the pole. The curtains are then hooked into the track rather than rings, and are opened and closed by cords at the side. The curtains hang below the pole so that the headings do not catch the pole when drawn.

FAR LEFT Cream curtains with a simple straight valance with a hand-gathered heading and small stand-up frill. The window here presents a challenge as it extends the length of the wall and continues round the corner with a balcony door. The clever solution was to extend the valance around the corner over the balcony door, but to keep the curtains at the window only for ease of access through the inward-opening balcony door.

Three sill-length wooden Venetian blinds hang at the wide window and a full-length blind at the door.

LEFT A close-up of the balcony door with the full-length blind and valance extending over it.

ABOVE The unusual Venetian blind in this London kitchen is made from both wood and metal slats. The blind is reflected in the mirrored wall.

LEFT Straight gathered valance with curtains all in a neutral-coloured checked fabric. The plain simplicity is the key to the charm of this children's bedroom in London.

RIGHT Dramatic wide-stripe fabric, again in neutrals, is used for the flat pelmet, curtains, headboard and bed cover to great effect. The window treatment is reflected in the mirror behind the bed.

BELOW Linen French-headed curtains hang from a fabric-covered lath with sheer curtains hanging on tracks fitted in the window recess. Both sets of curtains in this very wide-windowed bedroom are functional.

WINDOW TYPES

ARCHED WINDOWS

THESE BEAUTIFULLY shaped windows, often a feature in their own right, can be challenging for the curtain maker and fitter. The simplest option is to hang curtains on a track or pole fitted across the arch, so that the whole of the arch is seen by day but obscured at night. Fixed-headed curtains and fittings can be shaped to the curve of the arch and the curtains held open with Italian stringing or tie-backs. Shutters and arch-shaped blinds can also be used.

LEFT A magnificent Venetian bay window dressed with four curtains held by matching fabric tie-backs. The delicately fringed swags follow the shape of the Venetian window. Cream cotton twill under curtains hang directly behind the main curtains. When the room is not in use the under curtains are drawn to protect the furnishings from sunlight.

ABOVE Close-up of one of the finely ruched tie-backs, which is edged with a picot braid.

LEFT A view of one of a pair of arched windows in the same room, dressed with a similar swag arrangement to the Venetian bay window opposite. The swags are fitted above the arch so there is room for a straight, corded curtain track.

ABOVE LEFT Arch-shaped, goblet-headed, Italian-strung curtains with fan edging on the leading edges and central tassels at this corridor window.

ABOVE A straight window in the same corridor with matching goblet-headed curtains hung from a pole.

FAR LEFT Arch-shaped, goblet-headed Italian-strung curtains, knotted rope at the base of the goblets, central tassels, fan edging on hems and leading edges.

LEFT Close-up of the arch-shaped, goblet-headed curtain with central rope clover and tassels.

To Italian string curtains, rings are positioned at the back of the curtain where the curtain needs to be pulled back. To gather the curtains, cords are threaded through the rings and up to screw eyes, fixed to the window frame or pelmet board. Then the cords are wrapped around a cleat hook at one side of the window.

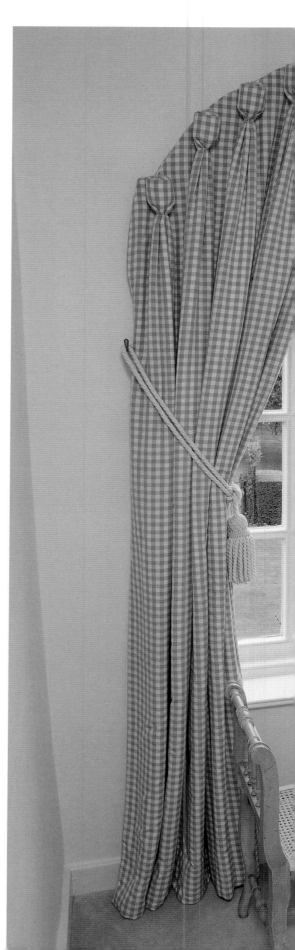

ABOVE AND LEFT A Venetian window with traditional working shutters.

RIGHT Goblet-headed check curtains with high tassel tie-backs at this arch-shaped half-landing window.

FAR RIGHT ABOVE Close-up of the arch-shaped goblet-headed curtains.

FAR RIGHT Light-weight cotton, hand-gathered curtains are fitted in the recess of this small arched window. The curtains are fixed simply with Velcro hook and loop tape, and held open by straight ties.

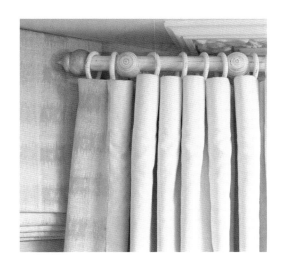

BAY & BOW WINDOWS

BAY AND BOW WINDOWS tend to be a focal point in the room as well as allowing in large amounts of light and creating a feeling of space. There are often other, straight windows in the room to be dressed in a similar style and matching fabric. Bay windows can have between three and seven windows, possibly a window seat too. But in general, any window treatment can be adapted to fit a bay, although shaped, possibly specially-made fittings, will be necessary.

LEFT Functional Roman blinds are fitted in the window recess so the window seat can be used by day and night. Full-length dress curtains hang at each side of the window; they soften the effect and add elegance.

ABOVE Detail of the box-pleated dress curtains hanging from a short pole with gold-painted finials.

LEFT Detail of the yellow check contrast binding on the leading edge of the curtain which matches the check Roman blind.

LEFT A wide bay in this family drawing-room. To avoid loss of light, a shallow flat pelmet was chosen, and the pelmet board was extended well beyond the window frame and around the side of the wall. Hence the curtains stack back on the wall rather than the window. The pelmet is deep only over the curtain stack-back area, again to minimise loss of light. The lower edge of the pelmet is softened with tassel fringe, the top edge is defined with plain-coloured cotton braid, and the seams are concealed by the same braid.

BELOW Detail of braid and fringe on the flat pelmet.

Heavy curtains in bay windows will need metal tracks that are specially bent for the individual window. Plastic tracks curve around bays quite easily and are suitable for light-weight curtains.

ABOVE Overlong curtains hang from a pole which has been fitted across the front of the window. The curtains are held back by tassel tie-backs. The inside of the bow window has been dressed with a swagged valance and Roman blinds behind. For continuity the window seat cushions and valance are in the same fabric as the curtains and the swagged valance.

RIGHT Self-striped velvet swags and tails trimmed with a tassel fringe hang at this country dining-room bow window. Small decorative tails are fitted at the intersection of the swags.

LEFT A small bow window with an attractive treatment. The window is fitted with a curved pelmet board and metal track. A charming gathered valance is hanging from the front edge of the pelmet board and is trimmed with rope and bullion fringe.

RIGHT Sill-length curtains in floral linen and cotton follow the shape of the window. They are finished with a straight, French-headed valance trimmed with knotted rope and fringe. The curtains leave the window seat area free by night and day.

BELOW Detail of the leading edge of the curtains with inset, linen fan edge which matches the rope and fringe on the valance.

A **picture rail** can interrupt the hang of the valance. Here, a narrow groove has been cut in the picture rail and the end of the valance has been slotted into the groove. A neat way of keeping a valance snug to the wall when there is a picture rail.

ABOVE A very small arched window in the same room as the bow window opposite. Boldly treated, the same valance and curtains as the bow window have been used. A checked blind with an arch-shaped lower batten fills the large expanse of wall space above the tiny arch window.

ABOVE RIGHT Full-length working curtains across the front of the bay, and working French-headed sill-length curtains round the inside of the bay.

RIGHT Detail of the pink fan-edge trimmed leading edge and hem which adds pretty definition.

LEFT A closer look at the French-headed sill length curtains hanging inside the bay. The French heading is ideal for a neat stack-back inside the bay. These internal curtains hang from a discreet, white, curved metal track which blends in well with the white window frame. For continuity the lined-only inner curtains are made up in the same beige fabric as the main, interlined, curtains and valance.

If the reverse of the curtains can be seen when sitting on the window seat, the curtains can either be lined in the face fabric, or a contrast lining for added interest.

DOORS

DOOR CURTAINS are not only practical curtains to keep out draughts and cold, particularly in older houses, but they can also visually frame entrances. They may be made up in heavy fabrics, and benefit from being interlined, providing the fittings can take the weight. The challenge is choosing fittings and curtain designs which allow inward-opening doors or French windows to be opened and closed unimpeded. A portiere rod can be fixed to the door itself or a track or pole fitted to the wall space above the door.

LEFT Gathered curtains in a delightful embroidered fabric and edged with a small cream fringe on the tops, leading edges and hems. The curtains hang from a pole and are held by tassel tie-backs. For ease of access, the wood pole has been placed above the door and extends beyond the frame.

ABOVE Detail of the embroidered linen curtain fabric.

LEFT Close-up of the double-tassel tie-back which was specially made to match the fabric.

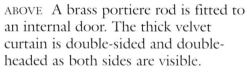

ABOVE A brass portiere rod is fitted to an internal door. The thick velvet curtain is double-sided and double-headed as both sides are visible.

TOP RIGHT When the door is closed.

CENTRE RIGHT The top of the curtain when the door is open, showing the brass device which allows the curtain to move with the door as it opens.

RIGHT Close-up showing how the hooks are sewn in between the face and the lining fabrics.

FAR RIGHT A shallow, check pelmet with onset, fringed swags and tails is fitted above this outward-opening garden door.

TALL & NARROW WINDOWS

TALL AND NARROW WINDOWS, rather like a tall slim person, are easy to dress and look elegant in almost anything. Simple or elaborate window treatments work equally well. One style particularly suited to this shape of window is fixed-headed curtains which are joined together in the middle and held open by either high tie-backs or Italian stringing.

LEFT Classic Italian-strung hand smock-headed curtains hang from a curved board. The curtains are damask-printed linen and cotton; they are finished at the centre with cotton rope and tassels and the leading edges are trimmed with a heavy, cream cotton bullion fringe.

ABOVE Close-up of one of the cream cotton central tassels.

LEFT Detail of one of the bullion fringed, Italian-strung curtains.

LEFT Italian-strung curtains, trimmed with tassel fringe on the leading edges hang from a straight board.

ABOVE A single curtain held open by a high tie-back and balanced by a short tail on the left-hand side. A fabric roller blind is fitted behind.

RIGHT Gathered curtains, joined at the centre, hang from a pole. They are held open by high rope tie-backs which match the fan edging on the curtain's leading edge. The fabric has an integral printed border which has been left showing only on the leading edges. A patterned roller blind is fitted behind.

WIDE WINDOWS

WIDE WINDOWS are often a feature in more modern homes and extensions, and have the advantage of not only letting in a lot of light but also creating a closer connection with garden and view. Understated window treatments and fabrics are often the best answer, so that the curtains are not overpowering. And should you decide to use a flat pelmet or valance, a serpentined lower edge gives a more interesting effect. A series of blinds is also an option.

LEFT Three goblet-headed curtains hang from a pole that extends the full width of the wall. The middle curtain is fixed at the centre, and pulls half to the left and half to the right. The plain cream curtain fabric blends in well with the wall colour. Relief is provided by the red felt tops and leading edges.

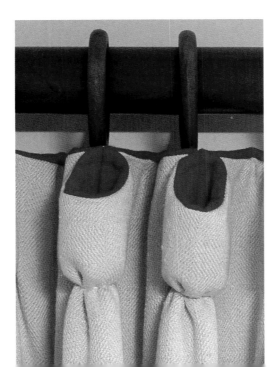

ABOVE Close-up of the compact wooden finial which suitably finishes the end of this very long pole.

LEFT Close-up of the goblet heading. The goblets have been scooped out and lined with red felt.

LEFT A series of four white, sheer Roman blinds cover a wide window in the dining room of this modern London flat.

ABOVE Simple plain, cream gathered curtains hang from an iron pole with a curly finial. Two pinoleum blinds, with black edging, are fitted in the recess.

Poles fitted at wide windows will always need a centre bracket as well as the side brackets to support the weight of the curtains and the pole.

ABOVE A serpentined gathered valance with onset trumpets, all trimmed with fringe at this wide, drawing-room French window.

FAR RIGHT Wide bedroom window with only a small amount of space above the window. A pretty gathered and serpentined valance softens the lines of the window.

RIGHT Detail of the gathered valance made from printed linen, and trimmed with plain linen fringe which is the same colour as the contrast-bound top.

SMALL & DORMER WINDOWS

SMALL AND DORMER WINDOWS need to let in as much light as possible. The options are either to blend the window in with the wall or to make a statement by dressing around the window. The former is simple and unobtrusive, while the latter makes the result more elegant. Dormers are small windows which project from the roofline, and may need special fittings.

LEFT A charming smock-headed valance with sill-length curtains held by tie-backs in this tiny bedroom in the country.

ABOVE A dormer window fitted with swing arms and double-sided curtains. The arms are hinged rods which enable the curtains to swing away from the window and lie against the side walls.

LEFT Another smock-headed valance with full-length curtains at this small bedroom window. The valance has been fitted on the wall space above the window and the curtains stack back on the wall space, either side of the window. Dressing the space around the window and using full-length curtains has made a feature of this small bedroom window.

ABOVE Full-length dormer, balcony window with working, double-sided curtains hanging from swing arms in the recess. Puff-headed, dress curtains are slotted onto a narrow brass pole which has been fitted on the sloping ceiling. The over-long, dress curtains are held open permanently by small fabric tie-backs. The full-length curtains make the most of the ceiling height and add elegance.

RIGHT A close-up of one of the slot-headed, double-sided working curtains hanging from a brass swing arm. When hanging full-length curtains from hinged swing arms, ensure that the arms and brackets are strong enough to take the weight.

ABOVE AND LEFT A classic solution for dormer windows. Cut-to-fit hinged brass rods with double-sided slot-headed curtains held by tie-backs. The rods can be pushed back to the wall, or closed across the window, the tie-backs can be removed at night.

FAR LEFT A close-up of the bracket and slot-headed curtain with stand-up frill above the slot.

ABOVE LEFT A buckram-covered, flat pelmet with a trimmed and shaped lower edge. The full-length curtains combined with the deep pelmet look impressive at this small bay window.

ABOVE Pretty chintz curtains hang from a fabric-covered track which has been bent round the dormer window.

LEFT Detail of the flat pelmet.

ABOVE A Roman blind fitted at this window set in the sloping roof of a converted barn. The blind is kept close to the wall by cords and rings at either side of the blind.

RIGHT A detail of the Roman blind when it is closed. It has a green contrast binding on three sides, and is in the same room as the sill-length chintz curtains on the opposite page.

A skylight is set at the angle of a sloping ceiling. Any curtains or blinds have to be kept close to the angled ceiling. Cords and rings or poles need to be used to do this.

MATCHING PAIRS OF WINDOWS

MATCHING PAIRS of windows are always pleasing, and add to the symmetry of the room. Rather like twins, they have impact simply because there are two of them. Broadly speaking, there are three solutions. Each window can have an identical pair of curtains; a single curtain only at each window; a central curtain covering the wall space between the two windows, with a single curtain on the far side of each window.

LEFT Matching pair of windows with fixed-headed, Italian-strung, box-pleated curtains hanging from curved boards. The cream curtains have a wide band of check fabric along the leading edges and hems and are finished with dark-blue fan edging. The tops of the curtains have a small contrast binding also in check. Check Roman blinds are fitted behind the curtains. A chest of drawers and picture above define the space between the windows.

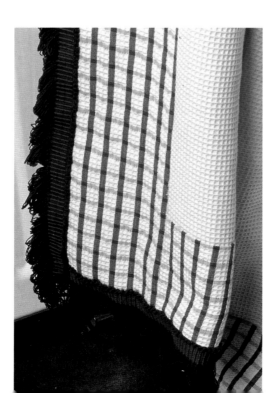

ABOVE Detail of check Roman blind and curtains with check border and dark-blue fan edging.

LEFT Detail of the check contrast-bound leading edge and hem, with dark-blue fan edging.

LEFT Matching windows with pretty, classic English chintz, curtains and gathered valances with serpentined lower edges trimmed with fringe.

ABOVE Single overlong curtains in brightly coloured silk, hang from white poles at French windows; they frame the large portrait well.

FAR LEFT Here, the matching windows have been treated individually. The pole finials are almost touching, arch-shaped valances are hanging from them with curtains behind. The column emphasises the separateness.

LEFT Single curtains, with attached valances, at alcove windows on either side of the chimney breast. They add definition to the fireplace.

ABOVE One pole has been fitted across the two windows, and the centre curtain when drawn covers half of the right-hand and also half of the left-hand window. The centre curtain is twice the width of the outer curtains. Three curtains is a good solution when the space between windows is limited. There is fringe on leading edges of the outside curtains and on both edges of the centre curtain.

113

AN ASSORTMENT OF WINDOWS IN A ROOM

WITH A VARIETY of window shapes, it is important to treat them with confidence. They can be unified by the fabrics and fringes, even if the actual window treatments are entirely different. When smaller windows are mixed with larger ones, blinds or poles are often the solution for the smaller windows. For windows of different widths, use the same top treatment but vary the width to suit.

LEFT A straight window and a bow window in the same room dressed with swags and tails. The solution was to have three swags hanging at the narrower straight window and five at the bow. As it was not possible to put the top of the swags in the bow at the same height as the straight window, the lower edges of the swags were put to the same height for uniformity.

ABOVE A picture of the whole of the bow window dressed with shallower swags than the straight window.

LEFT Detail of swag and tail trimmed with yellow fringe. The tail is lined in a plain yellow fabric.

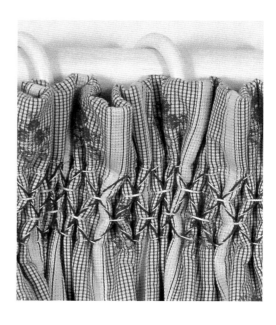

BELOW A large and small window in the same bedroom. The small window has a Roman blind made up in the same check fabric as the walls. This visually blends the window in with the walls. At the larger window the long curtains hang from a black pole and are made up in the same fabric as the walls and the blind. Although the window treatments are quite different, they work well together.

LEFT Two matching windows with smock-headed curtains hanging from curved boards and Italian strung. Roman blinds are fitted behind.

ABOVE A pair of curtains in the same room, hang from a pole, harmonising the look by using the same smock heading and fabric as the curtains hanging from the curved boards.

FAR RIGHT ABOVE Detail of the smock heading used as a unifying feature on all the curtains in the room.

Curved boards are made out of wood and can be 23-30cm (9-12in) deep at the centre. They work well on portrait-shaped windows up to 2m (79in) wide.

CURTAIN STYLES

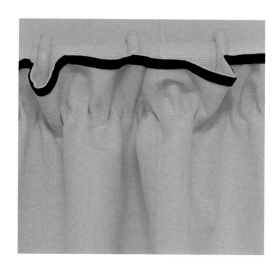

SIMPLE CURTAINS & SHEERS

SIMPLE AND SHEER curtains are popular for their very versatility. Surprisingly, they work well in both formal and informal settings. They can be used to counter opulence or soften furniture and architectural features with hard lines. Sheers are invaluable where you wish to filter light as gently as possible. They can either be used by themselves or in conjunction with conventional curtains and top treatments.

LEFT This challenging half-landing window has no wall space at the left-hand side. A single muslin curtain is hanging at the right-hand side and held by a large decorative hook. The leading edge and hem is trimmed with bobble fringe. The curtain finishes at the skirting board and is topped with a black velvet pelmet, cut away at the lower edge.

LEFT Unlined off-white linen curtains, hang from a pole, they softly filter the daylight. The simple curtains have an attached hand-gathered valance with a velvet-trimmed stand-up frill and tulip shaped lower edge.

ABOVE A close-up of the top of the attached valance trimmed with narrow black velvet ribbon.

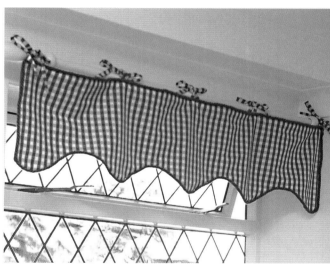

LEFT A single unlined curtain with very little fullness, and a small fringe on the leading edge and hem, at this bathroom window.

FAR LEFT A band of braid, trimmed with red lace, has been used as a flat pelmet and looped onto brass pins, at this stone mullioned window.

ABOVE At this kitchen window an almost flat gingham pelmet tied onto a pole. It has a scalloped lower edge and rope has been hand sewn on all sides.

TOP Detail of flat gingham pelmet.

FAR LEFT Two sets of gathered working curtains, the outer are unlined linen and the inner are muslin.

LEFT A detail of the headings of both the muslin and the linen curtains.

ABOVE Three Roman blinds fitted at this bay window. For privacy, flat panels of sheer fabric slotted onto narrow brass poles at the top and also the bottom, are fitted at the lower half of the windows. The striped sheer panels are simple and practical.

RIGHT Close-up of sheer panel.

LEFT Here, an unusual painted wooden bed corona with a sheer curtain simply hanging as a gathered panel behind the bed. It softens the strong lines of the bateau lit and completes the bedroom.

ABOVE A three-windowed bow where the windows have been treated individually. They are hung with over-long muslin curtains trimmed with fan edging and simple gathered valances trimmed with linen fringe.

The success of using sheers lies in using plentiful amounts of fabric. Three times fullness is a good rule of thumb for curtains and valances. To avoid seams in sheer curtains, purchase fabrics in wide widths.

FABRIC-COVERED LATHS

A FABRIC-COVERED LATH is a very small flat pelmet which conceals the curtain track. The fascia is made from either buckram or hardboard and covered with the curtain fabric; the gliders and curtain hooks move freely behind. It is a simple but smart treatment which can be fitted to both small and large windows, and works well in both modern and traditional settings.

LEFT A spacious bay window in this country bedroom had very little wall space above. The solution was an understated, cream fabric-covered lath and cream goblet-headed curtains with check contrast border inset with a fan edging. This permits maximum light through the windows onto the dressing table.

ABOVE Detail of the cream goblet-headed curtains with check border and inset fan edging which hang from a fabric-covered lath, shown in full on the opposite page.

LEFT French-headed check curtains hang from a matching check fabric-covered lath. A Roman blind is fitted in the recess. The blind is edged in the same check fabric cut on the cross.

LEFT Deep-gathered, striped curtains hang from a lath covered in the same striped fabric.

ABOVE A detail of the striped fabric-covered lath and gathered curtains.

RIGHT These colourful French-headed curtains hang from a fabric-covered lath. It was an ideal choice for this bright room because there was no wall space above the window for a top treatment. Maximum light is allowed into the room.

Curtains that are exaggeratedly overlong should be avoided with fabric-covered laths as they drag when pulled and will cause undue strain on corded tracks.

POLES

THERE ARE A WIDE VARIETY of poles, from wholly traditional to ultra-modern. They can be made from iron, wood or brass, and the finials provide a great opportunity for a stylish finish. The advantage of poles is that they do not restrict light coming into the room, particularly when the pole is extended beyond the window frame, so that the curtains stack back over the wall area. Poles are versatile and suitable for all shapes and sizes of windows.

LEFT These hand-sewn, French-headed curtains have been made up in a striped fabric. The fabric has been pleated to follow the stripe, this is only possible when they are pleated by hand as with tape the spaces are pre-set. The curtains hang from a beautiful wooden reeded and gilded pole.

ABOVE Close-up of the tassel-shaped finial that finishes the pole with a flourish.

LEFT Close-up of the attractive brass pole bracket and the brass rings.

RIGHT Goblet-headed curtain with an attached valance trimmed with wool bullion fringe and held by a wool tie-back, hangs from a mahogany reeded pole with a ball and point finial.

ABOVE Close-up of the hand-sewn goblet-pleated attached valance.

LEFT Trumpet valance with shaped lower edge hangs from a pole. The pole has been projected out in front of the curtain track by wooden blocks.

Attached valances are an ideal solution where a top treatment is required without loss of light but there is no wall space above the window. The valance simply moves with the curtain when opened and closed. Attach swags and tails for a more sumptuous look. Attached top treatments benefit from being fringed to demarcate them from the curtain.

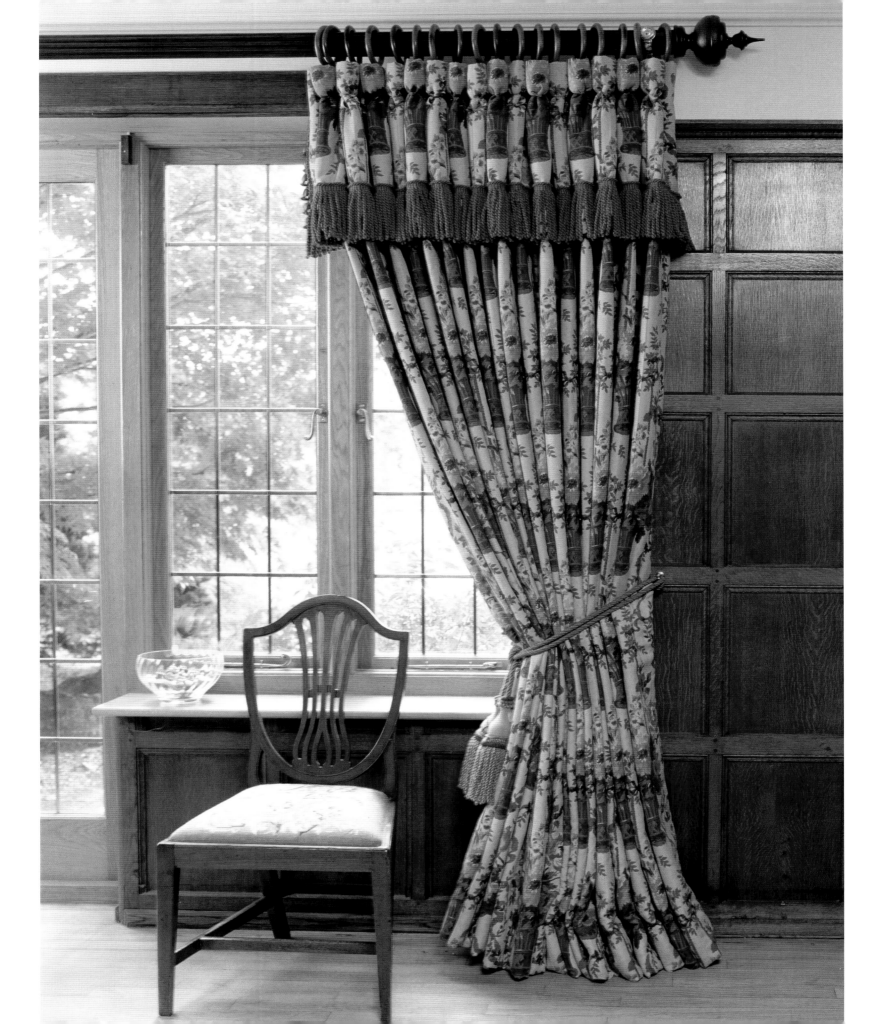

ABOVE AND LEFT A leather-covered pole fitted round the bay window. A curtain track has been inserted on the underside of the pole and the pole is supported by overclip brackets. The sheer inner curtains hang from a curtain track behind the pole.

RIGHT A wooden pole has been fitted across the front of this bay window. At night the full-length curtains can be drawn across. In the day the window seat can be used. The window seat cushion and valance are made up in the same fabric as the curtains.

ABOVE Discreet brass poles with gathered curtains are fitted at these three windows. The plain curtains have been trimmed with a striking braid set in from the leading edges and hems.

RIGHT Detail of ombra at another window in the same room.

FAR RIGHT Detail of braid trim.

ABOVE Goblet-headed large check curtains hang from simple wooden poles in this family sitting room. The goblets have been carefully positioned over alternate checks and have been made to the depth of the check.

LEFT A low-ceilinged dining room where the pole is fitted well above the small window.

Positioning poles requires thought. They can be fitted to the window architrave; on the wall space above the architrave; or fitted right up to the ceiling or coving. In older houses, the walls may not be strong enough to hold the brackets, and the architrave may be the only answer. If there is more than one window in the room, where it is sensible to do so, put the poles at the same height.

139

VALANCES

A VALANCE is a gathered or pleated pelmet which is hung from the front edge of a pelmet board, it conceals the track and curtain heading. Valances provide a soft, pretty effect and can be used in almost any room. Because the valance heading is fixed, all manner of headings can be employed. A useful device is to hang the valance in dead wall space above the window, thereby visually lengthening the window and at the same time allowing maximum light into the room.

LEFT These simple gathered valances with gently curved lower edges trimmed with dark red bullion fringe work well in this elaborate setting. Green-and-white, narrow-striped ticking roller blinds with a lace edge are fitted in the window recesses.

ABOVE A detail of the gathered heading of the valance. The gather line is narrow, and there is a stand-up frill above. The pelmet board is set below the cornice so that the cornice is not obscured by the top of the valance.

LEFT Detail of the bullion fringe that defines the lower edge of the valance.

141

ABOVE A smart, box-pleated valance with hand-sewn rope set down 6cm (2in) from the top of the valance. The lower edge is trimmed with fan-topped block fringe and the top is contrast-bound in red.

FAR RIGHT Lavish puff-ball valances in a printed moire fabric. They have gathered headings and frilled lower edges. The puffed effect is made by placing net inside the heading, rather like a net petticoat under a ball dress.

TOP Detail of the frill on the lower edge of one of the puff-ball valances.

ABOVE A single curtain with attached puff-ball valance works well with the larger windows in the rest of the room.

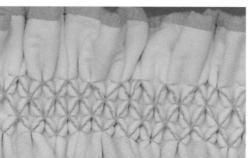

ABOVE A cream smock-headed,
serpentined valance with fringe.

RIGHT Detail of smock heading.

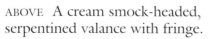

ABOVE A second serpentined valance,
gathered onto a flat buckram yoke.

RIGHT Detail of fringe on valance.

ABOVE A third serpentined gathered valance with a frill on the lower edge.

RIGHT Detail of pinked double frill.

RIGHT Two nearly identical windows hung with pretty double-pleated valances with scalloped lower edges and trimmed with cream fan edging. The pleats and flat spaces have been worked out to take account of the blue-and-white, toile-de-jouy print.

The proportions of a valance are vital to the success of the design. In a room with a low ceiling the finished length of the valance can be one-sixth of the curtain length. However, in a room with a high ceiling, the finished length of the valance can be one-fifth of the curtain length.

ABOVE A pair of matching windows with curtains and gathered valances hanging from elegant curved pelmet boards. The valances have contrast-bound tops and are trimmed with linen, block fringe on the lower edges. The width of the pelmet boards has been extended to balance the slightly narrow windows.

RIGHT Detail of the pink-and-white linen block fringe.

Lower edges of valances benefit from being defined by fringe or fabric contrast binding, to differentiate them from the curtain behind. If there is any shaping on the lower edge, that will be further emphasised.

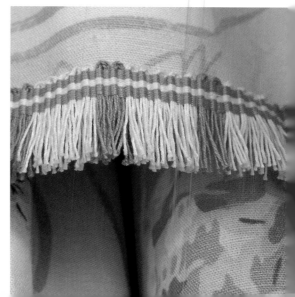

148

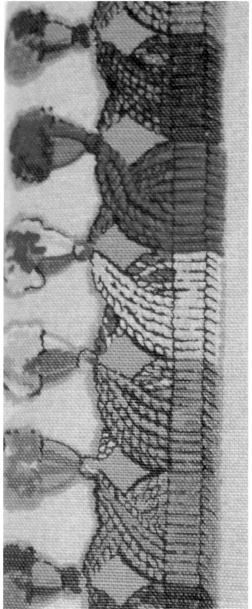

LEFT A gathered valance hangs from a scallop-shaped pelmet board, hand-sewn rope covers the valance gather line. The lower edge of the valance and side edges of the curtains are all finished with a printed tassel fabric border. This shaped pelmet board is highly effective on classic portrait shaped windows.

ABOVE Detail of the unusual printed tassel fabric border.

149

FLAT PELMETS

A FLAT PELMET is a fabric-covered band of buckram, canvas or plywood. Flat pelmets can be fitted to any shape of window, they can be fitted on the wall space above the window to elongate the appearance of the window. As they are flat, they are economical with fabric, yet at the same time, make the most of any pattern on the fabric. Lower edges can be curved or shaped geometrically.

LEFT A flat pelmet, with onset swags trimmed with fringe, at an inner-hall window. The top edge of the pelmet is defined by rope and a central rope bow and tassels. The curtains are held by bullion fringe tie-backs.

ABOVE Close-up of the jaunty, central rope bow.

LEFT Close-up of the long bullion tassel tie-backs.

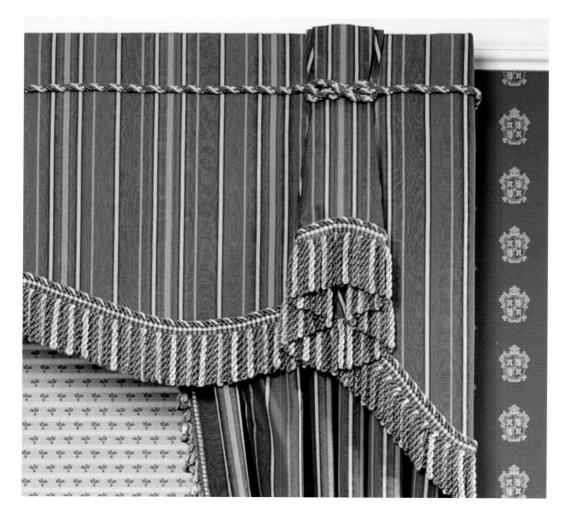

RIGHT A traditional study with smart striped curtains, flat pelmets and laminated fabric roller blinds. The curtains are trimmed with tassel fringe and held back by matching rope and tassel tie-backs. The flat pelmets have curved lower edges and onset trumpets, all trimmed with bullion fringe. Rope is set down 10cm (4in) from the top of the pelmet with knots at each coronet and trumpet.

ABOVE A detail of the onset double-pleated trumpet and coronet.

LEFT A close-up one of the double-tassel tie-backs which coordinates with the fringe on the leading edges of the curtains and the bullion fringe and rope on the pelmets.

LEFT A chenille flat pelmet that has been backed with canvas for a slightly softer look. The dramatic shaping of the lower edge is defined by rope and finished with tassels at the centre.

ABOVE Close-up of the central tassels and rope design.

The usual proportions for flat pelmets are one-sixth to one-eighth of the curtain length. The dramatically deep pelmet here is one-fifth of the curtain length.

LEFT These curtains and flat pelmet were made a hundred years ago from fabric, that was at that time, already a hundred years old. The classic style of both pelmet and fabric are still popular today. The attractive scallop-shaped lower edge of the pelmet works well with the design of the fabric. The pelmet board is bowed to follow the curve of the wall. This window is one of three windows in a curved bow.

ABOVE A close-up the antique chintz fabric and lower edge of the pelmet.

ABOVE A neat, straight flat pelmet, trimmed with fringe and sill-length curtains, held by tassel tie-backs, hangs at this wide dormer window.

LEFT An embroidered Indian panel was cut into two to make a pair of pelmets (one pictured) in this kitchen. The pelmet is trimmed with red fabric on the top and scalloped lower edge.

RIGHT A flat pelmet, with a zig-zag lower edge, and a blind behind. For an uninterrupted look, the cream-and-green topiary fabric matches the wallpaper, ideal for a small window in a small room.

FAR RIGHT Blue-and-white check flat pelmet with playful zig-zag lower edge in this child's room.

FORMAL SWAGS & TAILS

SWAGS AND TAILS are the ultimate way to dress a window, they are a grand treatment which is suitable for more formal rooms with higher ceilings. They look sophisticated when made up in beautiful fabrics and trimmed with fringe. Generally speaking, the wider the window, the more swags there are in a design. They are arranged to give the illusion of continuous drapery although each element is made up and fitted separately.

LEFT A three-windowed, Regency bay with a swag at each window and a tail and chou at the far edge of the side windows only. Tassels and choux finish the swags at the inside edges of the windows. An unusual swag and tail arrangement, combined with the pretty choice of fabric and a bold colour scheme, creates a wonderfully individual effect.

ABOVE Close-up of one of the fabric choux that has been used at the top corner of each swag.

LEFT Detail of one of the side tails which has been contrast lined in the same turquoise colour as the walls and trimmed with vivid tri-coloured block fringe, specially made to match the colours in the curtain fabric.

159

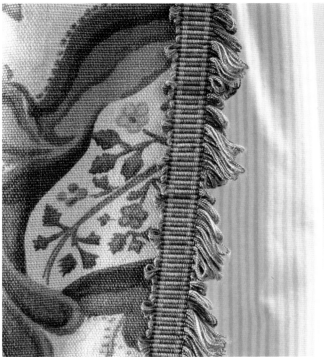

LEFT Landing window curtains with swags and tails. The tails have been contrast lined and double tassels hang at the intersection of the swags. For definition, rope runs along the top of the pelmet board. Here, the coving was brought up to the window edges only so that the pelmet board could be fitted right up to the ceiling to increase the curtain height. Also, the centre swag is shallower than the two outside swags; this allows more light onto the landing and creates a softer lower edge.

FAR LEFT A small arch-shaped hall window, using the same fabric and tassels as the landing gives continuity. Goblet-headed, Italian-strung curtains shaped to the arch allow more light in than swags and tails would have done. Knotted rope at the base of the goblets, central tassels and trimmed leading edges add finish.

ABOVE Close-up detail of the fabric, fan edging and striped lining.

LEFT Delicately-proportioned swags and tails hung from antique gilded cornice boxes. The curtains are made from old silk damask and the swags and tails and tie-backs are made from an old brocade-type fabric trimmed with its original fringe. The swags are finished at the centre with a spiral-shaped tail, also trimmed with fringe.

ABOVE Close-up of the central gilded shell on the cornice box.

RIGHT A view of the drawing-room wall with its dramatic row of three identical windows.

BELOW A Venetian window in the same room, dressed with curtains and cream roller blinds only.

ABOVE A magnificent dining room with three identical windows along one wall. Swags and long tails are draped over dark poles, with rope trefoils and double tassels at the centre. Cream striped moire laminated roller blinds hang in the window recesses.

RIGHT A detail of fringe on the tails.

FAR RIGHT A head-on view of one of the three windows.

164

RIGHT A matching pair of windows dressed with imposing swags and tails. Made from printed linen and cotton fabric, they are set onto a flat yoke and trimmed with cream bullion fringe. The dramatically long tails sit just above the dado height, and are lined with plain cream fabric to echo the fringe. Pleated coronets are placed at the top of the tails, and rope is knotted at the base of the coronets and runs along the base of the flat yokes. Fabric trefoils with rope and tassels are placed at the junction of the swags.

ABOVE A close-up of one of the pleated coronets with knotted rope.

LEFT Swags with trumpets, in a pretty chintz fabric and trimmed with short fringe, create a light treatment for the bay window of this country bedroom. The bay window has been treated as three individual windows rather than as a continuous whole.

ABOVE A close-up of one of the bows placed at the top of each trumpet.

The success of swag treatments lies in the use of pleasing proportions. To achieve a balanced look, swags and swagged valances should be one-fifth of the top of the pelmet board to the floor measurement. The tails should be either two or three times the length of the swags. To mock-up the position and depth of swags, put a length of chain against the window to form the arcs of the swags and outline the proposed design. Here, the swags are, unusually and deliberately, less than one-sixth of the curtain length and the trumpets are only slightly longer than the swags. This produces a delicate period look.

LEFT A matching pair of windows dressed with swags and tails attached to a gathered valance, in contrast check fabric. Central trumpets are finished with choux; bows complete the tails.

ABOVE A swagged valance (this is a continuous valance of swags with trumpets at the intersections) in a printed silk fabric, trimmed with block fringe and finished with rosettes.

BLINDS & SHUTTERS

BLINDS

BLINDS CAN be used either on their own as a simple treatment or in conjunction with curtains in a multi-layered treatment. Surprisingly varied, they are ideal for small windows, or windows where there is no space at either side for curtains. Blinds can be fitted inside the window recess or on the window architrave. They are economical with fabric, highly adaptable and work well in both traditional and contemporary settings.

LEFT Roller blinds made out of a chintz fabric, which has been laminated to give it sufficient stiffness to be made up into roller blinds. Small flat pelmets have also been made out of the laminated fabric and are fitted in the recess in front of the blinds to cover the tops of the blinds.

ABOVE Detail of the lower edge of one roller blind. The lower edge has a pretty cut-away shape at the centre. This cut-away shape is repeated in the shallow flat pemets.

LEFT Detail of the blind fabric.

FAR RIGHT A Roman blind made up in a printed linen and cotton fabric and set behind cut-velvet, tab-headed curtains which hang from a pole.

RIGHT Detail of the lower edge of the Roman blind and the leading edge of the curtain trimmed with a coloured jute fan-edge fringe.

BELOW Close-up of jute double-tassel tie-back. The curtain, as well as having fan-edge fringe on the leading edge, also has an inset, contrasting border of green cut-velvet.

ABOVE A metal Venetian blind hangs at this small window, in a small room. Black metal slats create a striking and modern effect.

RIGHT A metal roll-up room divider cleverly separates the kitchen from the eating area.

FAR RIGHT A Roman blind made up in black calligraphy fabric complements this elegant black, white and chrome contemporary kitchen.

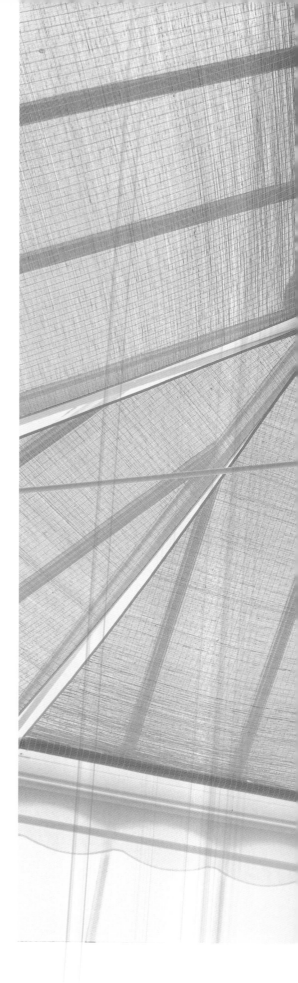

FAR LEFT Venetian blinds made from wooden slats that can be used either to filter or exclude light. They combine well with the check curtains.

LEFT AND ABOVE Two different conservatories both with made-to-measure pinoleum blinds fitted to the roofs, to filter light.

SHUTTERS

INDOOR SHUTTERS are usually made from wood and permanently fixed to the window. When closed, shutters give the secure sense of a barrier between the home and the outside world. When not in use they can be folded back. The caveat is that they can be draughty, and when they are combined with curtains and top treatments, ensure that the working shutters are not impeded by the other window treatments.

LEFT Louvred shutters provide an opportunity for fine tuning light coming into a room. They can be fully opened away from the window, or closed with light filtered by the louvres. When closed, the amount of light is determined by the angle at which the louvres are set. Here, for continuity, the shutters and woodwork have been painted the same colour.

ABOVE An unusual set of sliding sash shutters which are pulled from a box underneath the hinged sill. They are corded and balanced just like the sash windows behind them. An ingenious 19th century device which avoided the need for deep window reveals where side-opening shutters would be stored.

LEFT Another set of louvred shutters fitted at this kitchen window. They are combined with a carved and painted wooden swag and tail, which provides an individual finish to the window.

ABOVE Rustic shutters painted a blue-green colour to match the window architrave and sill. A charming feature in this utility room.

RIGHT Traditional shutters are just right here in this cosy sitting area of a country kitchen. The only curtaining required is this delicate, unlined broderie-anglaise valance, which is a pretty finishing touch.

Glossary

ARCH WINDOW A window with an arch-shaped top.

ARCHITRAVE The wooden surround to a door or window frame.

BAY WINDOW An angled window which projects from the wall.

BED VALANCE Panels of fabric or ruffles which cover the base of a bed.

BLINDS:
AUSTRIAN A gathered blind pulled up by vertical cords at the back; the hem falls into a series of scoops.
ROLLER A flat panel of fabric wound round a roller; a spring mechanism is fitted in the end of the roller.
ROMAN A flat panel of fabric which pulls up into horizontal folds by means of vertical cords.
VENETIAN Wooden or metal slats drawn up by a system of cords.

BLOCK FRINGE A cut fringe with alternate blocks of colour.

BOBBLE FRINGE A braid-topped series of bobbles used as a trimming.

BOW WINDOW A curved window projecting from the wall.

BOX PLEATS Fabric pleated to form box shapes. For an inverted box pleated heading, the box shape is put to the back of the curtain.

BRAID A narrow woven fabric used as a trimming.

BUCKRAM A stiffened calico used in curtain headings. Stiffened hessian, a heavier buckram, is used in tie-backs.

BULLION FRINGE A thick fringe with twisted hangers.

CHENILLE A velvet-type fabric with a looped pile.

CHINTZ A glazed cotton fabric often with printed floral designs.

CHOU(X) A decorative, round, hand-sewn, crinkly fabric trim.

CONTRAST BINDING Strips of contrasting fabric sewn onto the edges of curtains, valances, pelmets or blinds to define the edges.

CORNICE AND COVING Decorative or curved moulding placed where the wall meets the ceiling.

CORONA A semi-circular fitting used to hang curtains above a bed.

CORONET A fabric goblet placed above trumpets or tails.

CURTAIN HEADINGS The finish at the top of curtains. They can be gathered, pleated or even flat.

DAMASK A one or two-coloured, reversible, woven figured fabric usually made from silk or cotton.

DEAD WALL SPACE The space between the top of the window and the coving or ceiling line.

DECORATIVE TAIL A small, short tail which can be placed at the intersection of swags.

DORMER WINDOW A window projecting from the roof line.

DROP DOWN SIDES The outside edges of an Austrian blind which are not pulled up in to a scoop by cords.

DROPPED DOWN HEADING The frill above a gathered heading.

DRESS CURTAINS Non-functional curtains which do not draw.

FABRIC COVERED LATH Narrow pelmet board with a fabric-covered fascia fitted on the front edge of the board to conceal the curtain track.

FAN EDGING A braid where one side is looped to form a delicate, scalloped edge.

FINIAL A decorative round or pointed attachment, fitted at both ends of a curtain pole to contain the rings.

FLAT PELMET A decorative, fabric-covered band of buckram, canvas or plywood which is fixed onto the front edge of a pelmet board concealing the track and curtain heading.

FOUR-POSTER BED A bed with a frame which has a post at each corner and usually a fabric-covered ceiling.

FRENCH PLEAT Sometimes known as a pinch or triple pleat; it is a pleat with three folds in it.

FRENCH WINDOWS A pair of glazed doors opening on to a garden, terrace or balcony.

FULLNESS The relationship between the track, pole or pelmet-board measurements and the width of the ungathered curtain or valance.

GATHERED HEADING Narrow or deep gathers at the top of curtains and valances. They can be gathered by tape or by hand sewing.

GOBLET HEADING A pleated heading at the top of curtains and valances. The pleats are formed into goblet shapes.

INTERLINING A lofty, cream or white fabric which is hand sewn between the face fabric and the lining of curtains and top treatments. It improves the draping and insulating qualities of the face fabric.

ITALIAN STRINGING A decorative method of opening fixed-headed curtains using cords attached to the pelmet board. *See page 117.*

LAMINATED BLINDS Roller blinds made out of fabric which has been laminated to stiffen it.

LEADING EDGE The inside edge of the curtain facing the centre.

MULTI-LAYERED TREATMENTS Where two or more window treatments are combined at a window, say a blind, curtains and sheers.

OMBRA A decorative round fitting with a stem to fix it to the wall; used to hold curtains open.

OVERLONG Extra length, allowing full-length curtains to puddle comfortably onto the floor.

PELMET A generic term for any type of top treatment.

PELMET BOARD A piece of planed timber fixed to the wall like a shelf, used to fix curtain tracks to and also to hang top treatments from.

PINOLEUM BLIND A flat blind made out of bamboo split cane. It is pulled up by cords.

PIPING Cord sandwiched inside a strip of fabric, often in a contrasting colour, and inserted into a seam.

POLE A wooden or metal rod supported by brackets; curtains are hung from rings threaded on the pole.

POLONAISE BED A bed surmounted with a central dome.

PORTIERE ROD A metal pole fixed to a door. When the door is opened and closed both the rod and curtain hanging from it move with the door.

REEDED CURTAIN POLE A wood or metal rod which has a series of linear grooves in it for decoration.

RETURN The gap between the front of the window treatment and the wall. This can be covered by the curtain or top treatment for a neat finish.

SERPENTINED VALANCE Where the lower edge of the valance has a series of curves.

SHAPED PELMET BOARD Pelmet boards that have a curved or curved and shaped front edge.

SHUTTERS Hinged wooden panels fitted to the window frame; usually painted in with the window frame.

SILL-LENGTH CURTAINS Short curtains that finish either at or just below the window sill.

SMOCK HEADING A gathered curtain or valance heading which has been oversewn with embroidery thread, creating a honeycomb effect.

STACK BACK The wall area at the side of the window covered by the curtain. The curtain 'stacks back' or folds into this area when opened.

SWAGS AND TAILS The ultimate top treatment. Swags are scoops of fabric which are fitted along the front edge of a pelmet board. Tails are lengths of folded fabric, fitted at either end of the pelmet board.

SWING ARMS Hinged metal rods which are fitted at dormer windows for curtains to hang from.

TIE-BACKS Crescent-shaped fabric bands or lengths of rope which are used to hold curtains away from the window. Rope tie-backs can be finished with one or two tassels.

TRACK A metal or plastic rail from which curtains are hung. Tracks can have cording systems.

TREFOIL A three-pronged, fabric bow with a fabric-covered button at the intersection of the prongs.

TOILE-DE-JOUY FABRIC Usually on a cream ground cloth with a single-coloured pictorial print depicting figurative and pastoral scenes.

VALANCE A gathered or pleated fabric skirt hung from the front edge of a pelmet board or valance rail. It conceals the curtain track and heading. The lower edge can be straight or curved.

WINDOW RECESS The area inside the reveal of the window where blinds and sometimes tracks can be fitted.

YOKE A flat, often stiffened, band of fabric which is used above valances or swags and tails.

Other publications and services by Merrick & Day

THE ENCYCLOPAEDIA OF CURTAINS
An indispensable curtain-making guide with photographs and over 600 clear line diagrams and step-by-step instructions for making a wide range of different window treatments. With graded projects, from quick and easy to elaborate swags and tails; many techniques are explained here in this book for the first time.

THE CURTAIN DESIGN DIRECTORY 3rd Edition
Hardback and ringbinder versions available
A manual of black-and-white illustrations, with over 300 design ideas for curtains and soft furnishings. Easy-to-use Style Guide to identify quickly the appropriate window treatment. The twelve sections include Design Details, Poles, Valances, Bay, Tall and Narrow and Problem windows, Beds and Accessories. The ultimate guide to creative window treatments.

THE FABRIC QUANTITY HAND BOOK
Metric and Imperial versions available
Essential for anyone involved in curtain making and design. Accurate and easy to use for fabric, fringe and trim quantities. Includes quantity tables for curtains, valances, pelmets, swags, blinds, bed valances, covers, tablecloths etc.

THE SWAG AND TAIL DESIGN AND PATTERN BOOK
Everything you need to make beautiful swags and tails in one book. Over 70 swag designs to choose from, supported by make-up notes and full-sized swag and tail patterns from the Master Pattern Sheet.

SUPPLEMENTARY SWAG PATTERNS
To complement The Swag and Tail Design and Pattern Book, this Master Pattern Sheet contains eight swag patterns graded in size up to 170cm (67in) wide. The patterns and tracing paper are presented in a wallet.

PROFESSIONAL PATTERNS FOR TIE-BACKS
Patterns for plain, banana and scallop-shaped tie-backs each in 8 sizes. Clear step-by-step instructions. Presented in a wallet with tracing paper.

THE SOFT FURNISHING MASTER SYSTEM

Master Forms that can be photocopied and used or adapted. Contains measuring sheets for various window shapes, price list structure, forms for fitting and hanging instructions. The invaluable make-up sheets cover all types of window treatments and beds, plus accessories. Hugely practical, it is packed with time-saving forms.

LE PORT-FEUILLES PRATIQUE

Beautifully illustrated, black-and-white period curtain and bed designs, circa 1870, with clearly-drawn pattern shapes. This unique 26-page portfolio offers inspirational ideas from the past.

THECURTAINSITE.COM

www.thecurtainsite.com by Merrick & Day offers interior designers, decorators, curtain-makers and home enthusiasts information on curtain-making and design, fabric estimating tables for curtains and valances and a fabric companies and suppliers directory. Retail mail order service available for many hard-to-find curtain workroom supplies and sundries.

CREATIVE CURTAIN COURSES

Merrick & Day run a range of curtain-making courses in their North Lincolnshire workroom. They are based on practical tuition and offer a wealth of professional hints and tips, all in a friendly workroom environment.

MERRICK & DAY CURTAIN-MAKING WORKROOM

Merrick & Day offer a bespoke curtain-making service to interior designers and private clients. They specialise in hand-sewn curtains and top treatments.

MAIL ORDER SERVICE available from:

Merrick & Day Orders Department,
Redbourne Hall, Redbourne, Gainsborough,
Lincolnshire DN21 4JG England

Telephone: +44(0)1652 648814   Facsimile: +44(0)1652 648104
Email: sales@merrick-day.com   Website: www.merrick-day.com
www.thecurtainsite.com

All publications subject to availability

Index